Sandra Gurvis

Amherst, OH

Confessions of a Crazy Cat Lady

And Other Possibly Demented Meanderings

Loconeal books may be ordered through booksellers or by
contacting:
www.loconeal.com
216-772-8380

Published by Loconeal Publishing, LLC
First Loconeal Publishing edition: April, 2013

ISBN 978-0-9885289-6-3 (Trade Paperback)

Dedication

Dedicated to the dogs and cats, large and small, pesky and quiet whom I've had the good fortune to own, meet and be comforted by.

Table of Contents

Introduction

Why Am I Writing This Book?

Why does anyone write anything? Because we want to share, to enlighten, to provide a rationale for the day-to-day lunacy that often passes as life. And for me, I am also hoping that *Confessions of a Crazy Cat Lady* will serve as a gateway drug to my other books, including *Country Club Wives*, a recent satire about women, money and homeless animals set in "New Albany, oops New Wellington," Ohio and my as-yet-to-be-written "Geezerville" series about a certain large, extremely racially consistent retirement "Village" in Florida.[1]

Because *Crazy Cat Lady* is so cheap or, as my ex-mother-in-law used to say, "inexpensive," you might feel guilty or (more hopefully) entertained and purchase my other fiction/nonfiction titles, some of which are humorous, others not so much. Also you may not want to see me on the streets of Columbus, Ohio, pushing a shopping cart of books because I'm homeless and have no place to live because no one downloaded/purchased this book. But please, do not feel obligated to buy.

Additionally, people periodically ask me for copies of my essays, many of which originally appeared in *Columbus Monthly* and blogs. Not the cat ones; *Columbus Monthly* has never to my knowledge published anything about hacked-up

---

[1] Before you get all huffy about the "Geezerville" and "whitebread" references please understand that a "Geezer" is usually considered to be anyone 60 and over, so I qualify, and the same goes for my race. It's the gangster principle of self-deprecation. However, should you ever refer to me as "old," you will do so at your own risk.

hairballs, purring being interpreted as growling or tail in the face at 3 a.m. So some of the animal stories were in various small magazines and anthologies. But you'd have to dig really deep to find them; or at least I did because many were written a while ago and could only be located at the very bottom of my ginormous bin o' stored clips.

Which brings me to my next point. Why the footnotes and pictures? I have a couple of very talented humorists/essayists to thank for those ideas: Jen Lancaster for the first and Jenny Lawson for the second. I only hope to do their original concepts justice; plus they lend a certain je ne sais quoi to the proceedings. For those of you who don't speak French that means "I know not what" and according to the Urban Dictionary is especially applicable if you want to be all suave and debonair (pronounced de-boner[2]) to give an explanation of something of a certain unknown or indescribable quality.[3] I also took a few liberties with some of the earlier essays by revising them slightly and adding the aforesaid footnotes/photos, and I apologize in advance for the two poems in the cat section. I can't help it—at least I didn't get into the topic of my first grandchild. Well, not too much, anyway.

Anyway, it's time to get this party started. I'd like to thank the following for their help, encouragement and assistance, both now and in the past: Ray and Sherry Paprocki, James and Angela Barnes, along with assorted family members and friends. With regards to the last two, I tried not to be too embarrassing or unflattering when picking the pictures. And also my cats, past and present—especially

---

[2] Aka the exact opposite of a sex toy party, but not in this context.
[3] The Urban Dictionary's milieu recommendation is: "'This house lacks what the French may call a certain je ne sais quoi,' said the pretentious rich bastard."

Oliver, Teddy, and my two current bestie beasties, Sasha and Savannah. And also thanks to Melissa Connolly (http://melissaconnolly.blogspot.com) for her wonderful cover illustration and boundless patience—she sure knows how to make a girl and her kitties look good (for the record, the ones on the cover are closer to a lifetime cumulative total, rather than my usual two). Finally, my parents' dog Duke (or "Puke" as we lovingly called him because of his colitis) who died in 1972, and whose picture remained in my wallet until a couple of years ago when I misplaced it, along with my friends' senior class photos.[4]

Without further ado, here goes nothin' as my mom used to say. I hope you enjoy!

Sandra Gurvis
Columbus Ohio
December 2012

---

[4] Darlene, I was visiting you in California when that happened. WHERE ARE THEY???

Two-Legged Observations

The Perils of Middle-Aged Singlehood

"How long have you been divorced?" I asked Barbara, who stood next to me at the mixer.

"I've never been married," the attractive, elegant woman whispered, and at my surprised expression, continued. "Whenever I tell people this, I feel like I'm admitting to being an ex-con."

Well, I was married for 26 years and have been divorced for almost three, and I can relate. Being thrust into the world of middle-aged singlehood is like trying to get into a pair of thong panties. It feels awkward, looks even worse and hits you right where you're most vulnerable.

My first foray was a religious singles group. Although many people there were close to my age, they acted much older, and seemed resigned to fading gently into the world of gray hair, bad knees and visits to the MCL cafeteria. They were exuberantly friendly, but it was the kind of attention you get when you walk into a nursing home to visit an elderly relative.

Recently they sent me an e-mail inviting me to a program on "Changing Living Arrangements." What was next? I wondered. A field trip to the Cleveland Casket company?

Other well-meaning friends have suggested that I try online dating services, something called "It's Just Lunch!" and speed dating, which basically involves sitting down and talking to a member of the opposite sex for two to five minutes, stopping in mid-conversation at the ring of the bell and then moving on to the next potential soul mate. All of which had about as much appeal to me as cleaning the cat box. In fact, I'd rather do the latter because at least I don't feel akin to a single-family dwelling that's back on the market.

Finally, I found the Columbus Ski Club. This organization, which consists of both married people and singles, sponsors all kinds of sports activities, ski and other trips, parties and Friday happy hours at bars and restaurants. Since I love to play tennis and enjoy socializing, it seemed like a good match.

And it was. The people in my tennis league arranged to sit together at a Halloween party, which is where I finally met a single man I found interesting. Although the world is full of nice men, a good portion of them are married, and even if it's unhappily so, that's not a place I care to visit. This man was friendly and mentioned that he'd see me at the mixer the following week. We even knew some people in common.

The next few days were like high school all over again. Should I buy a dress or shoes? Would I recognize him? (Everyone had worn costumes.) Finally I settled on a new blouse, which seemed like a good compromise.

The fateful night arrived and the mystery man entered the room. I walked up to him with a big smile and started talking, drawing on my somewhat rusty flirting skills. When he excused himself from the conversation and said he would see me later, I remained unfazed, returning to my tennis friends and dancing. When it happened the second time with another promise about later, and he walked over to another table and asked a trim thirty-something with streaked hair to dance, I got the hint. I was devastated.

I wanted to go back to my apartment and cry. I felt as though I'd acted like a fool, although I knew on a rational level that I probably hadn't. Perhaps this was punishment because I'd been so picky about men and critical when my divorced friends ended up with guys who weren't interested in sex or had been married four times before. How I'd disparaged the well-to-do widow who looked the other way as her new spouse eagerly mingled his limited finances with her healthy bank account and investments.

Then I got mad. Who was this guy to reject me? I was hardly the desperate and dateless type, grasping at every chance to go out with anyone, wondering when I was going to meet a guy who would "take care" of me. No, thank you. I spent 26 years thinking that someone already was. I fully intend to take care of myself, spending every extra penny on getting certification as a medical writer and finishing two books.

Then I realized the situation was like seeing a great-looking leather skirt. Although it held promise on the hanger, once tried on, it was an unmitigated disaster. It wasn't the clothing's fault, or the guy's—although he could have used a little more finesse. At this point in our lives, most of us have an interior buzzer that goes off when we sense someone likes us. And there are messages—"I'm just getting over a relationship," "Gotta go, it was nice meeting you"—that you can send to save both parties' feelings. It seemed like he was stringing me along to stroke his own ego.

As my daughter-in-law pointed out, it was a good thing I discovered what he was like before things went any further. My son, always alert to the possibility of a quick buck, threatened to tell my ex and his new spouse about the debacle unless I gave him $20.

Hey, there are worse things than being alone—like finding a prince, only to discover that he's really a frog.

Word up, dog. The year before I'd gone to the Ski Club Halloween party dressed as a soldier which looked even worse than this.[5]

Didn't believe me, did you?

---

[5] Please see the next essay re: provenance of extremely sparkly gold purse.

The Purse-uit of Happiness

For women, the right purse announces to the world that you're fashionable and sexy, even if you'll never be mistaken for Naomi Campbell. I'm guessing it's sort of how guys feel about owning a Porsche or Corvette. In either case, the perfect purse (or car) says you've arrived.

Until a couple of years ago, however, I didn't understand that logic. I couldn't fathom why women would spend hundreds, if not thousands, of dollars on purses. For instance, my 28-year-old daughter, frugal soul that she normally is, thinks nothing of stopping at her favorite store in Chicago to purchase an expensive Italian number in some odd color (which, by the way, somehow always looks fantastic). Nor did I get why some women would give a few dozen dollars a month to one of two websites—bagborroworsteal.com and frombagstoriches.com—so they essentially could rent any purse they wanted, as long as they returned it in the same pristine condition it came in.

Then it all began to become clear to me when I saw the purse of my dreams in the window of Henri Bendel at Easton. Manufactured by a company called Charm & Luck, it was shiny and silver, crisscrossed with crystal-studded buckles and straps. I am drawn to anything that sparkles. I'm also drawn to men with beautiful hair, but, considering my experiences as a single woman, the purse is a much safer bet.

I couldn't justify, however, the three-figure expense. My exhausted credit card needed a little TLC. So instead I went to the Gap and bought a cute clutch for $39. I avoided looking in the window of Bendel on the way back to the car.

As it turned out, I had to return the Gap handbag, which was, among other things, too small. Purseless and walking past

Bendel again, I couldn't help myself. Like a grizzly following the scent of food in a trash can, I headed into the store to take a closer look at the Charm & Luck bag. It was gorgeous.

OK, so it cost $249 plus tax. But that purchase also was one of my happiest moments in recent memory, especially since the sweet sales lad wrapped in it a box with a bow and included a little "surprise"—a magnum of champagne. (It was an inexpensive brand, but still. . . .) And if spending that much on a purse was my first step toward becoming a "bag lady," well, so be it.

Everywhere I went after that, people raved about my purse. I felt like a celebrity. Then something strange happened. When I went to a travel writers' convention in Niagara Falls, a woman who lived near Las Vegas fell in love with my shiny silver crystal-studded bag. "How much?" she asked me. Rather than telling her the cost, I gave her the manufacturer's name and said she could get a similar one online or at a high-end store such as Nordstrom.

"No, I want that one," she insisted, pointing to mine. "How much will you sell it for?"

I thought she was kidding so I said, "Five hundred dollars."

"Fine," she replied without hesitation. She pulled out her wallet and peeled off five crisp $100 bills while the people sitting at our table laughed incredulously.

So what if I had to spend the rest of the meeting schlepping my stuff in a plastic carryall designed to hold press kits? Now I could afford two Charm & Luck purses. Instead, I later bought the same model in gold, which I loved even more, and pocketed the profit.

If someone had told me that an impulse purchase would have led to a 100 percent return on my investment, I'd have laughed in disbelief. But in a strange way, it makes sense—I followed my heart and took a chance. The same thing happened with my condo, which I bought several months ago when it practically fell into my lap. I've been thrilled with it since.

Of course, no one has offered me double the selling price . . . yet.

Step 1—Note glowing eyes in background (not demon, but cat Sasha)

Step 2—Out of the bag and onto the box!

Step 3—Bonus! It comes with champagne!

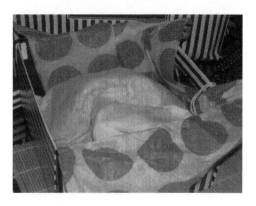

Step 4—Ahh, the anticipation . . .

The big reveal! (Don't judge . . . . It was 2005 . . .)

The Hard Drive/Hairdo Reset

I am sitting here writing this on a notepad because my laptop has crashed yet again, raising the depressing and costly specter of purchasing a replacement operating system. Besides, how else can I occupy myself for six hours while having my hair straightened? At $80 an hour for the Japanese procedure at City Cuts I should at least attempt to be productive.

Yet here I was, spending megabucks to compress my naturally curly locks into permanent flatiron submission. My quest to look like a brunette Peggy Lipton (remember "Mod Squad"?) started in childhood, with a hated pixie haircut. It lasted through adolescence, fielding assorted comments on my thick, unmanageable curlicues from "wild woman of Borneo" to "Brillo pad," although the latter is the hairstyle of choice today among women past a certain age.

By the time I reached college I was determined to have straight hair. My mother—perhaps out of sympathy or guilt for subjecting me to the unflattering-but-easy-to-care-for butch style of my grade school days—took me from salon to salon in search of the perfect hair straightening solution. Nothing took, despite various perms, pomades and promises; sure enough within a few short days or weeks, the frizzy curls were baaack, with a vengeance. So I resorted to the jumbo hair-roller/hours under the dryer/Dippity Do combo, which lasted about 15 minutes or whenever the humidity reached 75 percent. And in Ohio, the latter is almost always the case. I never did iron my hair, as the one time I attempted to iron anything—I think it might have been an apron in 7th grade in Home Ec—I set it on fire. And curly hair is better than first degree burns.

By the time I was married, however, I had bigger fish to fry than my hair. Like raising two kids and starting a career. So I went with the curls, and they did mellow with age like some fine wines. It was sort of a hair lowering compromise: I kind of learned how to style it—my hairstyling ability ranks only slightly above my talents in ironing clothes—and it became a part of me. Until my daughter Amy, who also inherited the family curse, decided to treat me to a birthday blowout at the Charles Penzone studio in Gahanna. *Her* childhood nickname had been "triangle head" thanks to an unfortunate Bat Mitzvah portrait.

"This is ridiculous," I told her as we walked into the salon. "You really should save your money."

"Trust me, Mom," replied my now 30-year-old, fashionable daughter whose hair always looks great, whether straight, curly or in-between, living proof of style over substance. "Worst case scenario, you can always wash it out."

When I saw the results, I was amazed. A smooth, sleek helmet replaced the stuck in the '80s mane which I'd worn for over a decade-and-a-half. I moved and it swung softly in the same direction, instead of going this way and that. It also made my face look different, although I couldn't figure out exactly why or how.

"Wow!" was all I could say. Suddenly I felt "hot." Not in the menopausal sense of the word but in the attractive-to-the-opposite-sex sense.

Then Amy informed me this amazing change could become semi-permanent with a safe and healthy procedure called Japanese hair straightening. The only catch: It costs about $600 including tip, give or take a few Ben Franklins, depending upon the texture, length, and type of hair. And it does grow out after several months, returning to the hair to its original untamed state.

At the time, I dismissed it as too expensive. Who would spend $600 for a new hairdo? But a few months later, on a whim, I decided to have my hair blown straight before a friend's wedding party. Much to my surprise, nearly early everyone at that reception came up to me and raved about my silky locks. Next to the bride and groom of course, I may have even been more talked about than the involved-but-not-with-each-other couple who were seen making out in the parking lot.

So I decided to take the plunge. Now, eight months later, in my second Japanese hair-straightening—they call it a touch-up, but it takes just as long as the first time—I came prepared with snacks, drinks, and laptop.

I would like say that my new hairstyle makes me look 20 years younger and the same amount of pounds lighter and turned me into a man magnet. But it was less than that, and also more. It rebooted my self-esteem and helped me become more optimistic. Every day is a good hair day—through rain, snow, sleet, hail, swimming pools, and sleeping on it weirdly. My hair is now far more dependable than any computer operating system. Which makes it worth every penny.

Pixie haircut plus awkward ballet pose equals hating parents as soon as I reach preteen years. It's amazing that this photo survives.

OK, so my hair was never really THAT curly. But you get the gist.

My official "straight hair" author photo

Here's another pic of me with straight hair. Actually my friend Liz has always wanted to be in one of my books. Congratulations, Liz!

Bonus/Worksheet:

20 Things That Are Worse Than Being Alone[6]

My Dad used to tell me, "You come into this world naked and alone, and you leave the same way." So one night, particularly disgusted after a conversation with a recently separated friend who immediately jumped online and became seriously involved with the first woman he met, I sat down and made this list.

Being alone is BETTER than:

1. Having a fatal disease
2. Having a chronic disease
3. Losing a child through death
4. Living in a war zone
5. Losing a sibling, parent or other family member through death
6. Losing a good friend through death
7. Being unable to support yourself (or losing a job)
8. Having a job you hate
9. Living in a place you hate
10. Having no friends

---

[6] I'm not saying that being alone is my first choice, but it beats the hell out of being with the wrong person or people. As Janice Joplin used to say, "Don't compromise yourself," although she probably took it to excess given her untimely death at age 27, which probably had more to do with ingestion of illegal and alcoholic substances than the desire for solitude. You're stuck with yourself no matter what, so why not make the best of it?

11. Having your children or relatives dislike you or not want to spend time with you
12. Spending time with people you dislike because no one else is around
13. Being in a relationship because there's no one else "better" (aka "settling")
14. Being in a relationship where someone's trying to change you
15. Being in a relationship with someone whom you hope to change, or you're trying to change
16. Losing a close friend through a quarrel, misunderstanding, or foolish pride
17. Being in jail or otherwise involved in criminal activity
18. Being a drug addict or alcoholic
19. Being sexually promiscuous or otherwise unable to really care for a significant person
20. Wanting to have a pet and not being able to have one
21. Not following your "bliss" and ignoring your inner voice and instincts

This list took me something like 15 minutes to compile and has 21, instead of 20 items. That's how easy it was. And you may have some of your own thoughts, so add them on the worksheet on the next page (or write them down on a piece of paper if you've downloaded the book):[7]

---

[7] OK, so this entry isn't particularly amusing and may seem pointless to some. But it really pisses me off when people feel sorry for those who are alone. Maybe we should pity them because they are stuck with some nasty, demanding, and gaseous individual who does nothing but complain and expect you to change their adult diaper. Who is better off, really?

Being alone is BETTER than:

_____

_____

_____

_____

_____

_____

_____

_____

_____

_____

_____

_____

_____

_____

_____

_____

_____

_____

_____

_____

_____

_____

_____

_____

My Life as a Traditionally Built Woman

It started in fifth grade. Well, probably before then, but fifth grade was the first time I remember being officially notified that I had joined the ranks of the less than petite. I'd gone to the doctor's office for a physical, stepped on the scale (hereafter known as Nemesis) and weighed 140 pounds, even though I was only 5 foot 3.

That's the only time I'll tell my real weight. Ever. And if you look at my driver's license, it says I weigh 125 pounds, which I actually did when I was 16. And as far as cashiers, cops and the world in general are concerned, that's the truth. After all, my hair is still brown, thanks to monthly visits to the stylist.

My mother, a size 6, was horrified by my fifth-grade weigh-in, although the doctor rationalized it as "heavy bones." Rightfully, Mother worried that I might take after certain family members whose "heavy bones" resulted in the tendency to be as wide as they were tall.

Around that time, the early 1960s, a woman named Jean Nidetch organized a group known as Weight Watchers, and I was enrolled when I was in seventh grade. My mother dutifully prepared (ugh) liver and onions every week per the diet's requirements. I was strictly counseled as to which foods were "legal" and "illegal." We also faced the Nemesis every week, in line, not unlike prisoners of war, watching as the person overseeing the process moved the balances on the scale before announcing our weight losses and gains—seasoning the diet with a dash of public humiliation.

In my teens and beyond, I was what they called a yo-yo

dieter, gaining and losing the same 15, then 25, then 35 pounds. Having two kids didn't help, either. By the time I was in my late 30s, however, I joined Jenny Craig and became more serious about nutrition, portion control and the right balance of foods. For many years I kept most of the weight off or at a reasonable level.

But then life interfered—a divorce, an illness of a close family member, menopause—and while I continued to eat healthfully, I wasn't so careful about portions. Sure, I exercised (walking, tennis, weight training and Zumba Fitness). I wasn't in a terrible clothes size and I thought I looked OK, although every damn camera that captured my image was distorted. And I refused to face the Nemesis, turning my back on it every time I visited a doctor.

Then several weeks ago I had a physical, and my doctor walked into the examining room, looking grim. I had specifically instructed her *not* to tell me how much I weighed. But when her first words were, "I know you don't want to talk about this," I knew I was screwed. After the number came out, 25 pounds higher than expected, I also heard "Weight Watchers" and the rest was "blah-blah-blah."

It would be nice if everyone would leave me alone about my weight. First my mother, now my physician! I like to eat, damn it, and was just getting comfortable with the whole traditionally built concept popularized by Alexander McCall Smith's *No. 1 Ladies' Detective Agency* mystery series. (For the record, I am far less traditionally built than the books' heroine, Precious Ramotswe.) But little things like blood pressure, cholesterol and heart disease need to be considered, and also the fact that most cameras are functional. And it might be nice to wear a bathing suit without a skirt that comes to my kneecaps (although bikinis aren't happening).

So that very night I went full circle and rejoined Weight

Watchers. The 21st century version is kinder and gentler, thanks to digital scales and declarations of group (as opposed to individual) weight losses. It's also a lot more flexible, with "Points Plus" assigned to foods based on protein, carbohydrate, fat and dietary fiber content. That makes it relatively easy to follow, allowing for reasonable portions of just about anything—although deep-fried Snickers and Texas Tonions still probably should be avoided. Exercise and physical activity are emphasized, also a good thing. And you don't even have to know your weight, as long as you quickly tuck your record of gains/losses into the back of the pocket guide provided to every member.

I've lost a few pounds—it's coming off really slowly— and have no idea what my goal weight will be. (Sometimes it's the journey and not the destination, right?) I now understand that I'll have to face my Nemesis every week. One day I might even purchase one and let it into the bathroom. But first I think I'll try bungee jumping or auditioning for "America's Next Top Model." [8]

---

[8] UPDATE: As of this writing (2012), I have lost about 35 pounds. I also recently bought a scale. But I haven't changed my mind about leaping from tall buildings or wearing skimpy outfits (see: "Ho, Ho, Humbug").

Me as a teenager/college student, next to my Mom. I thought I was "fat" in one of these but can't remember which! And yes, you have to turn the book horizontally to see this. But it's worth it for the cheap laugh!

Elvis had his fat phase. I had my "This camera is broken" phase. Geez, I even made the White House look small!

And then suddenly cameras become functional again!

Women and "Wives"

What is this obsession with "wives?" First came the Stepford Wives, a bestseller made not once but twice into a popular movie; "Desperate Housewives," which ran for eight successful seasons; and "The Real Housewives of [fill in name of major city here]" franchise courtesy of Bravo TV. Even my own novel, *Country Club Wives*, addresses this phenomenon.

"I think it's terrible and demeaning to women," observes my friend Lisa, a highly intelligent and successful computer software engineer. "Think about it—it sets us back almost 50 years. What the heck was women's lib for?"

Yeah, but . . . it's so much fun to get a glimpse into the lives of the rich and vapid, whose biggest problems seem to be to learn how to cook a chicken without first dousing it with dishwashing liquid ("The Real Housewives of Beverly Hills") or persuading the gals at the country club that you really can afford the ginormous house with the indoor/outdoor pool and tennis court even though you're single without any visible source of income ("Big Rich Texas," Style TV's offering in the genre). Discussions of and experimentations with various types of plastic surgery; shopping sprees and séances; trips to exotic places in the Caribbean, Africa, and Middle East can all be experienced by simply flipping on the TV.

Best of all are the fights and drama. Will Teresa from the New Jersey housewives toss another table (or her goomba of a husband) out the door, and how will Phaedra from the Atlanta franchise fare with her funeral parlor undertaking (no pun intended)? Even being kicked off/leaving the show can be parlayed into a new career; just look at Bethenny Frankel's multi-million dollar "Skinny Girl" franchise and her TV show, although somewhat less so with former archenemies Danielle Staub and Dina Manzo of New Jersey who became a stripper and an HGTV host, respectively. And then there's arguably the biggest failure/success in Housewives history, when former DC Housewife/Obama gate-crasher Michaele Salahi dumped her bizarre husband Tareq for Journey guitarist Neal Schon. And now they're engaged. Now that's entertainment!

OK, so my friend Lisa has a point. These shows hardly depict us women as the highly competent, intelligent, compassionate and productive creatures that we really are. But what about all those reality shows about bad restaurants, fashion disasters, child beauty pageants, over-the-top weddings, even not-so-fine art? There's something for almost every interest, taste and nationality. No matter what the platform, the same sort of silliness and undercutting goes on there as well. And yes, a lot of it is fast food for the brain and you do wonder what these people are really thinking when they talk into the camera (and whether you would do the same if it would allow you to quit your day job).

But for me, it's a chance to escape the humdrum of everyday life and reflect on how I would handle it were I that situation (not likely, but still a fun mental exercise). And you never know when an in-depth knowledge of wigs, Kelsey Grammer's odd personal habits, and designer show/charity event faux pas will come in handy. And if you get tired of one topic there's always something new, like the Bravo show on folks who give us those crazy Internet LOL cats. Pass the remote, please!

Shameless self-promotion alert! I was working on my novel
Country Club Wives *long before "Desperate Housewives" hit the*
airwaves!

Ho, Ho, Humbug!

The Saturday after Thanksgiving, I came home after an evening out when I saw that my neighbor had installed a ginormous, blinking snowflake on the siding of the townhouse directly behind me. That sucker (the snowflake, not the neighbor) generates a glaring kaleidoscope of gaudy colors in my bedroom window, reminiscent of the "Open All Night" signs facing flophouses everywhere, without the hefty monthly maintenance fee, of course. Since it gets dark early, I have to close all my blinds and shades so I can eat dinner without getting nauseous.

The next afternoon I met my son for lunch, and as I was turning into the restaurant, was almost T-boned by an antler-bearing car whose driver seemed so anxious to get to the adjacent department store that she forgot to look both ways. And I don't even want to discuss the large (in many senses of the word) group of diners who also wore antlers as well as blinking Christmas ornaments on their heads and seemed intent on making sure that everyone around them knew they were celebrating "the season."

I will spare you the other 797 reasons why the holidays annoy the heck out of me, because I know I already sound like a Scrooge. And there are some nice things about this time of year—discounts, pretty lights . . . um . . . hmmm. OK, let's move onto how to deal with holiday madness without becoming cranky, verbally abusive, or otherwise postal. For myself, I keep busy doing non-Christmas-related things and try to keep my sense of humor. I also stay away from situations that I know will light my fuse or be depressing . . . like going to the mall or, at times, going anywhere.

Which is why online shopping makes perfect sense. No fighting over items, pepper spray or shoving. And speaking of postal, you can avoid that mess altogether by purchasing stamps and labels online (www.usps.com). Use a Priority Mail shipping box or package, estimate the weight of the object, and schedule a pickup by the mailperson. On Black Friday, I decided to eat lunch at the same out-of-the-way restaurant that my friends chose for dinner that same night. Coincidence? I think not. This year, I'm sending my daughter a check for a pair of boots she's been coveting, while my son and his wife are getting Kroger gift cards because I receive quadruple points for discounts on gas. Now that's what I'm talking about!

TV ads get on your nerves? Thank goodness for DVRs. Don't have one of those? Well, Netflix offers a free month trial subscription for unlimited DVDs and streaming TV shows and movies. Just remember to cancel after the first of the year. Have nothing to do for Christmas or New Year's? There are plenty of people in the same situation, and they volunteer to help the homeless, Habitat for Humanity, and at food banks. Or they join meetup.com's various interest groups, which range from movies to yoga to hiking to—yes, even in Ohio—kayaking. There are lots of nice, like-minded folks who lack immediate and convenient access to huge families, large dogs, and elaborately ornamented houses.

Of course, I didn't get to this point easily or overnight. I've suffered through my share of lonely/depressing/sad holiday seasons, even when I was surrounded by my own extended family and my kids were young enough to be excited about the festivities.

But over the years, I've come to realize that the holiday season is a state of mind. It's like TV sports or Muzak—it's everywhere, so you can teach yourself to tune it out. (I was married for over two decades and have friends who are avid fans, so I've become a master at ignoring football). It also helps to understand that 'tis the banner season for marketers, retailers, and advertisers who want to push your buttons and encourage you to buy, buy, buy, whether it's out of generosity, obligation, or just to fill an emotional void. If they can make you feel inadequate or like you're missing out on something to sell their product, they will do so.

Last but certainly not least, the holidays only last a few weeks. Life returns to normal, and once again people start more or less abiding by the Golden Rule. But wasn't that the whole point of "the season," anyway?

These XXXXmas naughties were nicely discounted 30 percent at the Sears in Zanesville, Ohio. No one was buying though. That was because they were supposed to be shipped to Vegas . . . .

Of Melons and Men

Last summer, I rediscovered the joy of watermelons. And I was in luck, because the rainy spring provided a bumper crop. I also learned that 21st century watermelons can be had without the annoying seeds, adding that extra wedge of enjoyment.

So I spent quite a bit of time at the grocery store knocking on melons, trying to find the right one whose empty, hollow sound belied the treasure within. A yellow or cream-colored spot and a less than perfect exterior were also tip-offs to tastiness, according to a fellow melon hunter. And indeed, of the 20-some melons I ingested from June through August, all but one offered up slices of sweet, juicy pink paradise.

Then it occurred to me one day as I approached the melon bin, what if it was this easy to find a mate? Just walk up to someone, rap him/her on the head and listen for that telltale sound. While most people realize that extreme good looks rarely signal an equally fine or compatible personality, wouldn't it be easier if say, the prospect could also produce a slightly discolored, sort of reverse mark of Cain that guaranteed their wonderfulness? Think of how much money you'd save on dating services, crash diets, plastic surgery, purchase of that sexy new outfit, and dinner-and-drink fails. Of course, part of the economy might crash, but then farmers could make a fortune selling training melons a la practice tennis balls and teaching courses in "What Color is Your Rind?" a certain boon for any agricultural state!

Taking it one step further, you could also consider whether melons were under-ripe or not ready for a relationship. This would be someone who is underage, recently divorced, widowed, or just plain commitment-phobic. They might be a little too green. Knock on those and if you don't get much of a response, it's on to the next one. However, if you do happen to take one home, let it hang around for a while and see if it develops into something delectable.

With an exterior that gives slightly when pressed and a dull thud, the overripe prospect is the exact opposite. You'll find these bad boys at the top of the bin, rejects overeager for the first unsuspecting sucker who will take them home, break them open and find them rotten through and through. Sort of like a lousy Internet date or needy stalker whom you feel sorry for in a moment of weakness, they are best disposed of as quickly as possible. At best, you could hollow them out and use them to house other fruits or drown your sorrows by soaking them in alcohol.

Or you could search for the ideal specimen at the melon patch. What tastes better than a melon picked fresh from the vine? Just like first love, you know it's "virgin" and just for you without the baggage of being transported to the grocery store and handled by dozens of other prospective customers, not to mention being lugged around in gross-smelling trucks, rubbing rinds with those other grimy loser melons. But there are drawbacks to this as well. Unlike their vetted brethren, they may contain bugs and/or may be picked too soon, sort of like eloping with your 14-year-old second cousin. With melons, harvesting usually occurs after around 75-80 days when its tendrils turn brown; with people it's not so clear-cut.

According to some gardening sites, an immature watermelon is smooth to the touch, while one that's ripe has slight indentations or serrations that come with age. Heavier melons are also better, which bodes well for those of us with a few extra years and pounds. Farmers also advise patience when growing and selecting watermelons, also good dating advice.

My mother always picked the best watermelons and taught me the finer points of this art—and I also think it is a talent. She was equally astute when it came to my father— they were happily married for over 50 years, rarely spent a night apart and died within months of each other. Unfortunately, I did not inherit her ability or perhaps timing in the mate-selecting arena, but then, this is a different era and generation.

Melons, however, remain unchanged—even though some no longer have seeds. It gives me comfort, because maybe someday somebody will come knocking for me. Figuratively, of course, because I sure as hell won't be waiting for someone to thump me on the head, nor will I be the thumper. Until then, I have the reassurance of knowing that next summer all those luscious, ripe watermelons will be there for the picking. And I will be pounding on them until I track down the finest one in the bunch.

The perfect specimen . . . for my mother. My father, Dr. I.R. Goldberg, circa 1944.

Four-Legged Musings

Copy Cat[9]

Most days when I write, I drop off my three-year-old daughter at the babysitter's. Sometimes I wonder if I should include my Persian cat, Oliver. Anybody know the going rate for feline daycare?

Oliver can become a becomes a Class A pest when I'm working. He lounges on my notes, bats my correction tape into the den, hiding it among my daughter's toys and sheds all over my "invisible" tape. The latter totally destroys my copy, because when I'm writing a feature article, it's cut-and-paste city and the tape's "invisibility" hardly encompasses long, silky, black cat hairs. And when he's not trying to distract me, he snoozes in the cat-sized typewriter case or under my feet. Ever tried typing on a tight deadline with a live foot-warmer? A nice principle, but it's more like wearing slippers that keep moving around at will.

So why do I put up with all these cat-astrophes? Truth be known, Oliver can also be a source of inspiration. And we sort of suspected what we were getting into when we acquired

---

[9] This was one of my first "real" essays written in 1981 when my daughter Amy was three. It was also penned—literally—using notepads and then a typewriter (for those unacquainted with those ornery contraptions well-deserving of their obsolescence, please see the accompanying photos). Unfortunately Oliver and his sister, Patches, died of feline leukemia at the untimely ages of 7 and 5, respectively. Back then, people were far less cognizant of veterinary health and screenings than they are now. But some things never change. While Oliver was what LOL cats today call a "basement cat" and a Persian, my current Himalayan, Savannah, a white "ceiling cat" does many of the same things. Reincarnation? The circle of life? Revenge from beyond the grave? It's anybody's guess.

him—or did he acquire us?—five years ago on a crisp November night.

My then-husband and I decided to purchase a purebred feline because a previous kitten from a pet store had died of distemper. "The breeder told me she had a silver female and two black males," I said. "I definitely don't want a tom—they're mean and spray all over the house."

He agreed, adding, "Black cats give me the creeps."

We arrived at the breeder's house and the silver female was proudly displayed. But she shrank from my touch and fled in terror under the coffee table.

"Let me get out this black male. He's a real character." the breeder understated. She then presented Oliver, a huge fluff ball with blue saucer eyes who immediately began to purr, a sound so loud and grumbly that friends later interpreted as growling. The breeder placed Oliver on the sofa, so he decided to explore. But his mission was soon detained when he caught his claw on the pillow. Rather than being rattled, he simply looked at me as if to say, "Would you please remove this slight inconvenience?"

My husband and I exchanged glances. "We'll take him!" we chorused. Who could resist such a challenge?

The ensuing years have been cat-aclysmic. I quit my full-time executive job, gave birth

to a beautiful daughter and took up writing as a profession/high-risk gamble. Oliver's been there observing my progress—or lack thereof—a fat black meatloaf of an animal whose saucer eyes had turned a tiger orange but whose calm demeanor remained unchanged.

When things get bad—like my 75th rejection slip—he hangs in there, a silent sympathizer. He keeps me company at 4 a.m. when, cursing and frustrated, I'm searching for the right word or phrase. Who else would listen as I read the fifth revision of a paragraph aloud?

And who else would let me know that six straight hours of work is too much, and it's time to put food in the bowl? Punishment for noncompliance can range from a tail in the face at 3 a.m. to methodical dismemberment of the white feather centerpiece on the dining room table. And what other feline would pose for these pictures and the next day, stand with his paws on the typewriter hoping for yet another photo? And I didn't even have to bribe him with treats!

Although he can be a trial, Oliver is worth his weight in Tender Vittles.[10] If nothing more, he's a cat-alyst to the creative process who helps purr-fect my copy. So, are you going to stand there with that rotten tomato or actually throw it?

---

[10] Decried as the pet equivalent of junk food, Tender Vittles, a semi-moist cat food that came in convenient packets, was discontinued in 2007. It was loaded with sugar and salt and was said to contribute to obesity and bad breath which is probably why cats liked it so much (they're not so different from us). So now it's either canned or dried food and/or Party Mix and Temptations treats in a dizzying array of flavors. If your cat was born before 2007 and was all or nothing with Tender Vittles, you are SOL and have my deepest sympathies.

Oliver, waiting for inspiration—or perhaps an aberrant toddler— to strike.

Oliver hard at work on his own tome, "50 Ways to Hack Up Hairballs."

Man's Best Friend

By "Dennis" as told to Sandra Gurvis[11]

He sits at the top of the stairs, a fat gray-and-cream Buddha, surveying his kingdom. His name is Teddy, and he's got the world by the tail. But he's an insult to males everywhere.

Five years ago, my wife Laura begged me to purchase him. A Himalayan kitten would cheer her up after the birth of our third daughter, Sara. I acquiesced, partly because I was secretly disappointed Sara wasn't a boy and felt guilty and partly because I figured a purebred cat would have a little more class than your average feline. Laura also said that, with four women in the house, Teddy would provide me with much needed male companionship.

Now I know better. The only thing that differentiates Teddy from other cats is a certificate of registration from the Cat Fanciers' Association and an even greater hauteur. And the only thing we have in common is testosterone. When the girls aren't dressing him up in doll clothes, he'd off in some corner asleep or grooming his unmentionables. Or he's in Laura's office climbing on the bookshelves and meowing because he can't get down. And he always purrs, even when he's annoyed. What an idiot!

I want a dog. As the only true man of the house, I need a strapping, hearty canine for friendship and romping through the woods. Dogs are straightforward, honest, direct. They're

---

[11] OK, so it's obvious that this thinly veiled account is ripped from true life. I mean how many Himalayan cats in the mid-1980s were named Teddy? Fortunately however any identifiable parties have either passed on, moved away or reached their full adult growth.

always there for you, and you know exactly what they are thinking. None of this pussyfooting around and putting on airs. And they don't shed, leaving little "pieces of Teddy," as Laura puts it. At least not the Boxer of my dreams.

We've discussed getting a Boxer after Teddy uses the last of his nine lives. Although the two older girls, Jennifer and Heather, shudder at the misunderstood canine's homely and fierce (but so kind and loyal) mug, I'm sure they'd grow to love him, just as I did when I was a kid. Laura wonders who will walk the dog down our dark and deserted street when I'm out of town or want to go to bed early. She pointed out—and rightfully, I supposed—that she already has three children and doesn't want a fourth who, in a sense, remains a child all his life, dependent on his master. I replied that a dog is protection personified, and the children can help care for him. "Well, maybe a *little* dog," she relented. Sara said she'd love a puppy.

But Teddy is disgustingly healthy and cats live an average of 15 years. So I content myself with visiting my friend, Ed, who raises Boxers. Occasionally he offers me a free puppy and heartbroken, I turn him down. "Maybe someday," I say, "when the girls are older and Laura's not so stressed out . . ." Like when the kids are off to college and we don't want the responsibility.

Then, one day Teddy disappeared during Sara's sixth birthday party. With 15 first graders running in and out of the house, the door was constantly open. Although the cat never attempted to leave before, apparently he picked that afternoon to take a stroll. I thought I glimpsed something gray and white slinking through the woods as I pumped water into the Slip 'n Slide, but was too busy watching the kids to give it much thought. Besides, I couldn't possibly be that lucky.

We didn't realize the cat was missing until after midnight. Laura was so upset she woke up the girls and quizzed them about Teddy's whereabouts. No one had seen Teddy since that morning, when he was hanging around his half-empty bowl, demanding fresh refills with icy blue eyes.

The search mounted by Laura and my daughters rivaled "America's Most Wanted." They posted signs with the cat's picture and our contact information on telephone poles and in grocery stores. The entire neighborhood was put on alert. Laura placed an ad offering a reward in the suburban and city newspapers. Jennifer and Heather took turns calling the Humane Society every hour, while Laura berated herself because she'd failed to implant an identification microchip into Teddy when he was a kitten. But the moron was an indoor cat, so who would have thought he would have needed it?

After two days, I began to hope. Teddy wasn't coming back and although I wished him well, I'd miss him about as much as a toothache. I started to make surreptitious plans for a "surprise" from Ed's next litter. I'd call the dog Duke—after John Wayne—and he'd meet Laura's requirement for something small, at least for a few months. By then she'd be as attached to him as I was.

On the third morning I was getting into my car to go to work. I heard something faintly resembling a meow from behind the freezer in the garage. Oh no, I thought, it couldn't be. "Teddy?" I inquired, my stomach sinking.

The meow grew louder and more insistent. "Are you back there?"

I pulled the freezer away from the wall and there he was, huddled and dusty, balled in a corner. He looked terrified, his dignity shattered and instinctively I picked up and cuddled him. He licked my face but forgot to purr.

I know what you're thinking. A real man would have taken the cat away. The wife and kids would have never known the difference. I could have secretly located another home for Teddy, although he'd never receive the level of adulation he gets in my house. A reality check would have built his character; maybe even turned him into an actual pet, instead of the feline equivalent of a lounge lizard. And I could finally get my dog.

"Laura, look who I found," I called as I opened the door.

"You didn't!" she cried, tears streaming down her face. "Oh, Teddy!" But she gave me a big kiss.

Teddy jumped out of my arms and sauntered towards the empty food bowl. Lifting his tail, he glared at me because after all, I was standing between him and his cat chow.

You ungrateful wretch, I thought. A couple more days behind that refrigerator and you'd be indistinguishable from the debris that's already back there. And you know it, too. "Feed the damn animal," I ordered Laura. "I'm already late as it is."

There's one person in my house who's a bigger fool than Teddy. And he's not female.

The only "boxer" you're ever gonna have will be in your undie drawer!

Teddy: The Second Half

Your fur smells of whatever,
Your gentle demeanor belies a lion who attacks my ankles at
5 a.m.,
Your touch, once firm and unfearing, is now as tentative and
insubstantial as a child's,
Purring, a warmth, a solid devotion,
Your constant presence provides nameless comfort,
Like myself, you dwindle gradually,
I dread the void when you are gone.

Teddy, a LOL cat before his time.

Blindsided By Love

When I was growing up, we had the most thoroughly neurotic cocker spaniel that ever lived. Duke was a beautiful dog, but his bark overrode any good qualities that I might vaguely remember. He went into a seemingly vicious frenzy anytime anyone came within ten feet of our front door. Yet, decades later, I still carry his picture in my wallet, a reminder of a time when things never seemed to change and death was not an option.

Duke had colitis and my parents had a clear division of responsibility. Daddy walked him nightly, while Mother cleaned up after his "accidents" on the carpet. I couldn't figure out why my usually impeccable mother just didn't get rid of Duke. Who needed a gaseous, noisy embarrassment who scared away my high school and college friends and caused my parents' bridge partners to wrinkle their noses and glance suspiciously at each other?

The summer I was 21, I returned from a disastrous job experience on the East Coast. Totally distressed over a broken romance and a weight gain of a few pounds, I failed to notice Duke's absence when I came into the house. After listening to me complain for a several minutes about my miserable summer, Mother suddenly burst into tears. "How could you be so insensitive?" she demanded. "I put Duke to sleep three weeks ago and you never even asked about him." Oops.

When our children were young, I persuaded my then-husband—who claimed to be a dog person, but not so much when it came to nightly walks and cleaning up messes—to allow me to adopt a Himalayan kitten. The first breeder I visited had two eight-week-old males, Teddy and Freddy. I took one look at Teddy and that was it—I'd found my feline soul mate. Even his name was perfect—lovable, beautiful, and totally without purpose or utility, a sort of live stuffed animal that you could carry around for years (as my children did, with great enthusiasm). Teddy immediately took up residence on the chair of my home office. He had decided to let us stay in his new kingdom.

Teddy's bizarre actions belied his regal bearing. When he was three, we found him huddled behind the refrigerator in the garage after we'd given him up for lost. An indoor cat, he'd slipped outside and gotten confused. That was his first life. He was fond of sticking his head inside a potato chip bag (Teddy was also a slut when it came to Cheerios, pretzels and especially baloney). He meowed very loudly during our Passover Seder because he couldn't figure out what the singing was all about. My daughter Amy dressed him up in doll clothes and put sunglasses on him and he purred. I swung him around and danced with him and he purred and looked annoyed. My son Alex used him as a bull's eye with rubber bands and he didn't purr, but waited until Alex was petting him to take a nip of skin.

My husband forbade him to drink from the toilet but Teddy managed not to get caught. Nevertheless he (Teddy) willingly posed for pictures, and we have several of him on top of the commode, legs on the outside, paws on the inside, just about to dunk his head. Yet when people came over, he sauntered into the room and waited for them to remark upon His Gorgeousness before he left. The individual who failed to praise was met with an icy blue stare. Teddy also was quite the diva about mealtimes. If you mixed up the food (canned only, please) and pretended to put new stuff in, he'd show you the feline version of "talk to the hand"—only with his backside.

He was also a whiz at disrupting my work. This could range from sitting on the precise piece of paper I needed in spite of scores of others on my desk to jumping on the phone and disconnecting the caller, usually business-related and important. Teddy also liked to curl up next to the fax machine, which meant lots of cat hair to jam the insides, requiring yearly maintenance (of the fax, not Teddy, who like all cats was self-cleaning). He walked across it, turning it off and on at will. Still his presence was always a welcome distraction and mostly he curled up next to me, keeping me company.

Like Duke before him, Teddy symbolized the growing-up years, an era when there was little peace and every quiet moment spent stroking his luxurious fur and cuddling his vibrating body was treasured. He was there during the personal and professional triumphs and failures so common to a struggling writer and a growing family. So when he was diagnosed with kidney failure at age 9 (his second life), I felt angry and cheated, as if the curtain had been dropped before he'd had a chance to finish the play. Although the specialist half-heartedly suggested a transplant which would involve out-of-state-travel and thousands of dollars (Me: "Teddy and I are flying to California, where's he's going to wait for an appropriate donor. We can use Amy's college fund, right?" Husband: "Send me a postcard, because you're not coming back."), he did put the cat on a special diet and a regimen of medication. Having lost pets to disease before, I wasn't optimistic, although the specialist said he might live a maximum of three more years.

Amazingly Teddy rallied. He gained weight and returned to his zany self. But, also like Duke, he began having accidents all over the house. And like Mother, I cleaned them up and was put in the position of having to defend him against my husband and teenaged children who, although they still loved him, were disgusted by the messes. Teddy's third life came up for option during this period, when the exterminator changed the formula of the bug spray he used inside the house. The cat developed a tick and almost seemed to go in a coma. But once we figured out it was an allergic reaction, the vet said Teddy would recover when the spray evaporated. Which Teddy did.

The downhill slide (his fourth through ninth lives) was so gradual that I hardly took notice, not that I wanted to anyway. My husband commented on Teddy's increasingly slow gait and Amy remarked how thin the cat had become. Even Alex moved his target practice to our other two felines, Cleo and Sasha. But Teddy's eyes were bright and his appetite and hearing were good and his devotion to me remained unwavering. So I brushed aside the observations and ignored the cat's groans when I picked him up and his lack of agility and continuing accidents.

The issue of Teddy seemed to arise whenever I went out of town, which was fairly often. Eventually I had to board him (Teddy, not my husband)[12]. Whenever I came back, my husband would say, "You know, Sandie, this cat's about had it." Then I'd beg off one more week or two and no decision would be made. When I brought the subject up among my friends, one stated that she'd basically had the same situation with her childhood dog. "My parents ended up putting Fifi in the basement, even though he was blind and couldn't climb the stairs. They kept saying, 'He's all right; he's not suffering.'" When I looked into Teddy's eyes, I didn't see pain either, just love. And how could I in good conscience put my best friend to sleep?

Yet another trip came up and because of a time constraint and convenience, I had to leave Teddy with our family vet,

---

[12] That came later, and is the subject of another book entirely.

instead of the doctor who specializes in boarding cats. The animal who came back to me was slow and indifferent. Even so, on the way home he managed to open the automatic car window with his paw. He'd stopped eating, purring, and cleaning himself. He smelled terrible and his weight had to have been less than three pounds. Even the other two cats avoided him. Yet I held on for several weeks, giving it a few more days, hoping that he'd rally as he'd done in the past. And of course, I blamed myself for this latest reversal, if only I'd left him at the cat doctor, where he'd fared so well before. The vet said that I'd know when the time was right, but he hadn't counted on me being blindsided by love.

Like my mother, I did everything in my power to prevent that final, empty-armed walk out of the vet's office, which is the hardest part of pet ownership. But I finally had to. And when, really is the "right" time to let go?

Duke, our clinically insane yet strangely lovable cocker spaniel.

Teddy, kicking ass and taking names, even as a kitten.

Caught on film #1! Classic toilet bowl pose—Can I drink now?

Caught on film #2! And yes, Teddy could extricate himself as well.

Cowabunga! The Story of "Goldy"

On February 15, 2002 a cow escaped from a meat packing plant in Cincinnati, eluding capture for 11 days. Her plight caught the imagination and hearts of locals, garnering national attention and sympathy in a city torn by racial strife and providing welcome distraction from world terrorism and celebrity mishaps. Here is her story.

Call me Goldy. [13] At least that's what some of them did, along with Moo-sama, Heidi, Bossy, and Madame Charolais (after my breed). But Goldy suits me just fine, because that's the exact color of my hide, especially when the sunlight hits it just right. And if I'm going to be compared to some two-legged jerk, it might as well be Golda Meir, who at least did something productive with her talents.

I've heard that I'm bad-tempered, mean, stubborn, and just plain dangerous. But what would you have done, had you been in my hooves? I mean, if you had to choose between becoming someone's meat loaf or leaping over that six-foot fence? (No one can figure out exactly how I accomplished this, but I will tell you I did quite a bit of puissance on that farm in Kentucky. Horses aren't the only ones who can practice jumping over hurdles and being as I'm free-range, I'm not closely supervised).

I tried to warn the others, but they refused to listen. All they herd, er, heard was "cattle call" and stampeded right onto

---

[13] Ok, so my maiden name was "Goldberg" but that has nothing to do with the choice of name for this story. And "Goldy" was the nickname given to me by my college boyfriend and a few others. But the cow's obsessive behavior and antidisestablishmentarianism contrariness reflects the spirit of the late Golda Meir. Honestly!

that truck. Then they were too busy chewing their cuds about the lousy conditions, weird smells and udder matters to notice that their final destination was, well, final.

Besides, I had darn good reason for wanting to escape. The minute I arrived at Ken Meyer Meats, I knew it was bad news, especially since it involved humans. From the time I was a calf, they sought me out each year to "palpitate" me, which for you human females is about as much fun as your average pelvic exam. Even worse, when I was about a year old, the farmer led my mother away and I never saw her again . . . . None of the other cows would discuss it, but when one of us is "put out to pasture" it hardly means she's been herded to a better place.

But what really pushed me over the edge was Valentino. He was our resident steer and I must say, I am a sucker for long horns, curly eyelashes and a smoo-th ululation. And boy, did he know how to low, telling me I was the only one and that we would be together forever. Then one day I discovered him in the field cavorting with five other bovettes. But I really can't blame them. Horns do tell a lot about a man and he was only one around for miles. And they don't call 'em bulls for nothing.

So I decided to make a break at the first opportunity. As soon as I cleared that fence, off I went, running as fast as my flanks could take me. I weigh about 1200 pounds, give or take 150, but it's mostly muscle, which I plan on keeping, thank you very much. And since we were so close to that big park—I noticed it on the ride over—I steered myself in that direction. OK, so I stopped some traffic and ripped up a few lawns, but what is that in the overall scheme of things? Dumb humans were worried I'd attack their grocery stores and shopping malls. As if my goal in life was to forage for ground round and leather shoes. Nor am I interested in becoming a hood ornament on someone's SUV.

Eluding capture was a breeze. People are so noisy and conspicuous. They'd crash through the underbrush with their video cameras and on horseback and I'd stand there quietly chewing my cud and chuckling. They put food and water out, and I'd snag it when they turned their backs. Not to mention the dogs and helicopters which trumpeted their every move. Some steak, er, stakeout!

They brought in professional wranglers, veterinarians, and some organization called the Society for Prevention of Cruelty to Animals, which at first sounded suspiciously PC but which I later found out saved my hide. At least the cow catchers were up front, saying that if I was their animal, I'd get it between the eyes. But when one of them hit me with a tranquilizer dart, I showed him who's bossy and put the "live" back in livestock by dragging him around the park a few times.

But the most absurd ploy was the decoy cows, which they placed in temporary pens, in hopes to lure me back into the fold. All those girls did was gossip about my chutzpah, warning me to stay away. They also played pin the tail on the park ranger when the humans weren't looking.

Finally I got tired of the whole brouhaha. I had been on the lamb, I mean, lam over 10 days and although people will tell you they brought me down by roping me, tranquilizing me several times, and then loading me in a trailer via a Bobcat bucket, some lady named Marge called the final Schott.[14] Yes, I'd heard about the mayor granting amnesty and offering me the key to the city and some guy from a television show "Survivor"—What would he possibly know?—saying I could crash on his farm with his other animals. There was even a TV

---

[14] Marge Schott passed on in 2004. Unlike Goldy, however, her final destination is unknown.

deal in the works, an ad for a home-equity loan. But the possibility of refuge with a woman who owned a baseball team and then allowed her Saint Bernard to poop in front of thousands of fans at Riverfront Stadium really moooved me.

I let the public think that they won the battle by putting up a fight—towing my captors down McAlpin Ave. and through someone's back yard before my final cowpitulation. And I certainly became adept at fielding questions from visiting reporters by lunging and making threatening noises from my trailer before heading off to temporary headquarters at Miamitown.

But then this artist, Peter Max, offered me sanctuary in New York. I knew I'd found greener pastures, for both myself and other creatures when he donated paintings worth $180,000 towards the SPCA. Although I firmly nudged aside an appearance with him at the Cincinnati Reds opening day parade.

Now I await a new life, with other like-minded animals and possibly even a few eligible males. Heck, I might even be able to teach Oprah a few things about milking a bad situation for all it's worth.

Here's a random shot of my granddaughter, Hope. I swore I would never be one of "those" grandmas. I lied.

The Zen of Sasha

Follows are some reflections on my cat Sasha's 17+ years. We got her for our son Alex's 13th birthday present. She has endured a broken marriage, Alex's devastating illness and now, blessedly, the birth of Alex's and his wife Rian's daughter: my granddaughter Hope. Whenever my daughter Amy or even my ex-husband comes to town and drops by, it's old home week for Sasha—she remembers them and starts purring, no matter how much time has passed. One could learn a lot about forgiveness from Sasha.

Live in the moment
Be content
Keep yourself clean
Work just enough so you can sleep in a ray of sunshine.
Let it be known when you need something
Go outside when it's really nice
Accept your leash, er, limitations
Be willing to explore, but . . . (see previous item)
Purr loudly, except when you're being ignored (and then create havoc)
Throw up, if you must
As long as you have food, water, a bathroom and a loving "forever" home, it's all good!

Sasha being Zen

Confessions of a Crazy Cat Lady

I had very little experience with cats as a child. To me, they were small, pointy-eared little aliens with whiskers that my mother proclaimed to be "sneaky" as well as aloof and unaffectionate. I also heard that all cats caught and killed mice and other live critters and brought them into the house. Pretty gross, as such tales usually involved one or more bloody or decapitated "love offerings" carried by kitty into the bedroom or kitchen.

But when I was a senior at Miami University, I moved into a house with several other girls. My boyfriend at the time and his roommate were living with me temporarily until they found a place. I also wanted a pet, but the hamster that was boarded with another friend who'd stayed in Oxford over the summer met an untimely and disgusting end when her pets somehow figured out how to open its cage.[15]

A dog was out of the question, as a brief, disastrous experience the year before had culminated in the puppy pooping in front of my Archeology professor, much to the hilarity of the entire class.[16] My housemate Sue had adopted a kitten from a litter and suggested I do the same. I thought, OK, I wanted a pet, kittens are cute, why not? As it turned out, I ended up spending my life with felines, rather than the boyfriend who moved to England, got an unlisted phone

---

[15] Don't ask. Illegal substances were involved and the details were never made quite clear to me.

[16] What do you do with a puppy when you live in a dorm? Answer: Take it with you when you're not in the room, especially if you want to impress the cute guy sitting next to you in Archeology class. Or so you think until you realize that, instead of being something the parents took care of, the dog is your responsibility and you have no clue what to do with it.

number and eventually refused to talk to any of us after graduation. What-ever![17]

After college and much to my chagrin, I had to leave my beloved Bertha Butts behind with my other housemate, Jenny.[18] The future was uncertain; I'd hoped to follow the boyfriend to London but ended up living with my parents for several months. Eventually, however, I got a job and moved to Columbus. I also acquired two new cats, which proved to be yet another bad decision given my wacko roommates, frequent moves, and generally unstable lifestyle until I met my first—probably only—but now ex-husband.[19] The kitties, called Nirvana and Tribble, one of which I claimed to be seeking[20] and the other which oddly resembled those fluffy beasties from the famous original Star Trek episode "The Trouble with Tribbles," both met sad ends. Nirvana escaped during a roommate disaster and I was too overwhelmed to search for him; and Tribble, who was easily my favorite, slipped unnoticed out the door on a bitterly cold January morning a couple of months later. Neither was seen again and I always felt that losing Tribble was karmic punishment for abandoning Nirvana. A harsh lesson indeed and a mistake that was never repeated.

We had other cats and assorted pets throughout those first hectic years of our marriage and the kids' growing up. There were the goldfish: One died the morning I left town to

---

[17] This might explain why I'm a serial pet owner, rather than a serial dater/marry-er. It just seems a lot easier to adapt to an animal's weirdness and issues rather than a human's. Plus cats smell better and rarely fart.

[18] See footnote 15 above re: the cat's naming. Bertha, however, had a long and happy life with Jenny and her family.

[19] Why don't I use his name? How would you like to go through life with a moniker like Bozo Gurvis? Just kidding!

[20] A leftover from college hippie days, which I rapidly abandoned once I realized I actually liked making money and buying things.

interview singer David Lee Roth;[21] my seven-year-old daughter Amy was tasked with the obligatory burial at sea aka "swirly gate flush." The eventual demise of its surprisingly long-lived companion was caused by its (the fish, not Roth) continually getting a rock stuck in its mouth. Try explaining fish rock extraction as a reason to borrow your neighbor's tweezers and/or why you show up at the vet's office with the entire bowl in tow. There was the time when the kids' grow-a-frog committed suicide by jumping into the kitchen disposal when my husband was cleaning its aquarium, or so he claimed. And the rabid hamster, which I knew had issues from the "git-go." Amy, then 10, pleaded with us to adopt it, so we did. It latched onto her hand as she transferred it into its ball and my husband threatened to drop kick the thing into the next county unless I immediately removed it from the premises, so I ended up offering to actually pay a nearby pet store to take it.[22] I have had lousy luck with hamsters and under no circumstances will ever be involved with one again, even if my granddaughter Hope begs me. And that's final.

Alex, too had his share of odd pet experiences. A turtle which completely disgusted me with its gross, smelly habitat—tolerable in your human son but not in a cold, slimy thing that lives in a shell.[23] A rabbit brought in against my husband's wishes which lived in the basement for a while—Alex begged and begged me for it and unfortunately the ex

---

[21] This was big stuff, as it was 1986, during the height his wildly popular MTV videos and the aftermath of the Van Halen breakup. And no, he did not wear bottomless pants to the interview and is much better looking on stage than in person. Which may not be saying much, according to some people.

[22] Hear that, Nirvana? I always try to keep my word. Of course I have no knowledge of what they did after they accepted the hamster.

[23] Come to think of it, that last phrase also kind of described Alex as a teenager.

sometimes had to play "bad cop" because I was the resident softy. And several lizards and bearded dragons, strangely but extremely popular among middle-school boys. Whenever we went to Captive Born Reptiles to get the live crickets or whatever it ate, the place was mobbed with up-and-coming suburban aspiring gangsters. African-American and Asian kids had better things to do, like study or make the varsity sports team.

The dust settled, the kids grew up and moved out and so did my husband. And I was left alone with two cats, Sasha, who I still have and Cleo, who had shown up twelve years earlier at my husband's office shortly before his 40th birthday and the onset of his midlife crisis/personality transplant.[24] Sadly, Cleo passed away a few weeks before my divorce became final, so Sasha and I were on our own in the suddenly huge and vastly silent house. Since the soon-to-be ex had forbidden me to even think about getting another Himalayan, that's exactly what I did and Savannah burst on the scene. She was a nervy little diva, despite her petite stature—full grown, she's just shy of seven pounds. From the moment that tiny kitten curled into a ball next to me in my terribly empty bed, Sasha and I knew our place in the pecking order.

Now I am accustomed to and comfortable with being alone and the cats are still here. For as long as I can, I will have two feline companions. While they say cats are like potato chips and you can't have just one, I also say that two's company and three's a herd. Just like my children, who also own pets, they've got my back and I've got theirs.

---

[24] For the record, the ex has always claimed to HATE cats. For years, he gave the excuse of owning them as a deterrent to a detested ex-brother-in law who was allergic to felines, when in fact his sister had been divorced for decades. Okaaay . . . .

Alex, age 13, with Sasha as a kitten—love at first paw

Amy, also 13, with Teddy. Her hair looks SO much better now. Really.

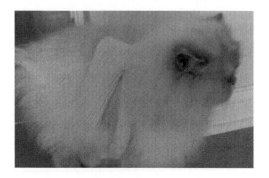

Savannah, the sock totin' Himalayan!

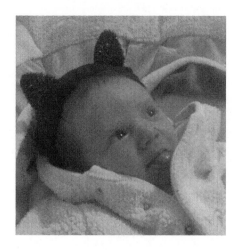

Baby Hope's first Halloween—Cat lady in training!

Sandra Gurvis (www.sandragurvis.com) is the author of sixteen books and hundreds of magazine articles. Her titles include DAY TRIPS FROM COLUMBUS, 3rd ed.; CAREERS FOR NONCONFORMISTS, which was a selection of the Quality Paperback Book Club; AMERICA'S STRANGEST MUSEUMS; and more. Among her recent titles are OHIO CURIOSITIES (Globe Pequot, 2nd ed. 2011), and a second novel, COUNTRY CLUB WIVES (Loconeal, 2012). She is working on two more nonfiction books for Globe Pequot: MYTHS AND MYSTERIES OF OHIO (2014) and JERKS IN OHIO HISTORY (tbd).

In the past, a major aspect of her work had been on the Vietnam protests and their aftereffects, resulting in two books, the novel THE PIPE DREAMERS (Olmstead) and a nonfiction title, WHERE HAVE ALL THE FLOWER CHILDREN GONE? (University Press of Mississippi) as well as a Web site, www.booksaboutthe60s.com.

While Sandra has had short stories and essays published in magazines, newspapers and anthologies, CONFESSION OF A CRAZY CAT LADY is her first collection of such work. Her newest projects include LIFE DURING WARTIME: A VETERAN SON'S ADDICTION, a memoir/guidebook that is currently in the developmental stages. She is also planning a "Geezerville" series of satires based in certain retirement "Villages" in Florida. She lives in Columbus, Ohio.

For more information visit her website, www.sandragurvis.com; her Facebook pages www.facebook.com/sandra.gurvis, www.facebook.com/pages/Country-Club-Wives/103644326397112; or find her on Twitter: @CCWivesNovelist.

VISIT THE LOCONEAL BLOG AT

www.loconeal.com

Breaking News

Forthcoming Releases

Links to Author Sites

Loconeal Events

Printed in Great Britain
by Amazon.co.uk, Ltd.,
Marston Gate.